Ten Po
about R

Candlestick Press

Published by:
Candlestick Press,
Diversity House, 72 Nottingham Road, Arnold, Nottingham NG5 6LF
www.candlestickpress.co.uk

Design and typesetting by Craig Twigg

Printed by Ratcliff & Roper Print Group, Nottinghamshire, UK

Selection and Introduction © John Greening, 2023

Cover illustration © Hugh Ribbans, 2023
www.hughribbans.com

Candlestick Press monogram © Barbara Shaw, 2008

© Candlestick Press, 2023

ISBN 978 1 913627 09 6

Acknowledgements

The poems in this pamphlet are reprinted from the following books, all by
permission of the publishers listed unless stated otherwise. Every effort has been
made to trace the copyright holders of the poems published in this book. The
editor and publisher apologise if any material has been included without
permission or without the appropriate acknowledgement, and would be glad to be
told of anyone who has not been consulted.

Thanks are due to all the copyright holders cited below for their kind permission:

Jo Bell, *Kith* (Nine Arches Press, 2015). John Wedgwood Clarke, *Landfill* (Valley
Press, 2017) by John Wedgwood Clarke. © John Wedgwood Clarke 2017. David
Constantine, *Collected Poems* (Bloodaxe Books, 2004) www.bloodaxebooks.
com. Carolyn Forché, *In the Lateness of the World* (Bloodaxe Books, 2020) www.
bloodaxebooks.com. Lorna Goodison, *Goldengrove: New & Selected Poems*
(Carcanet Press, 2017). The poem is reprinted by kind permission of Carcanet
Press, Manchester, UK. John Greening, poem first published in this pamphlet.
Anna Robinson, *The Finders of London* (Enitharmon Press, 2010). David
Wagoner, *Traveling Light* (University of Illinois Press, 1999). Susan Wicks, *Night
Toad: New & Selected Poems* (Bloodaxe Books, 2003) www.bloodaxebooks.com.

All permissions cleared courtesy of Dr Suzanne Fairless-Aitken
c/o Swift Permissions swiftpermissions@gmail.com.

Where poets are no longer living, their dates are given.

Contents

Introduction

You only need think how many words we've collected for *waste, junk, scrap, refuse, litter, landfill, trash* to realise how central it is to our lives. And poets have been writing rubbish poems – in the best sense – since long before Cowper sang the praises of his compost heap.

If Eliot's *The Waste Land* doesn't really count, AR Ammons's book-length *Garbage* certainly does, though no extract quite seemed right. We do, however, have part of John Wedgwood Clarke's sequence *Landfill* and all of Carolyn Forché's 'Report from an Island' to remind us that poems of protest can be lyrical. Forgotten decaying 'stuff' can disgust or attract. Laurence Binyon's 'The Burning of the Leaves' is about a wartime bonfire; but really it's an elegy and an invigorating vision of change. By contrast, the late David Wagoner elevates his Pacific Northwest garbagemen to mock-heroic heights – and is thoroughly entertaining. In Jamaica, meanwhile, Lorna Goodison finds a more serious spirituality, hymning "kings and queens of homelessness".

I could have filled these pages with house-clearing laments – though few so heartbreaking as David Constantine's irresistible 'House Clearance' – but preferred Susan Wicks's acute still life of a simple swing-bin. Then there was the professional angle: things we might call rubbish are "small finds" to ex-archaeologist, Jo Bell, and equally exciting for poet-mudlark, Anna Robinson, who hears an exotic music (a ghazal indeed!) in London's leftovers. Alas, we couldn't bring you James Fenton's 'The Skip', but his poem is a tour-de-force worth seeking out. As for my own contribution, it's a playful sonnet with an allusion to Larkin's 'As Bad as a Mile' (poets do like to recycle) about my wife's litter-picking, but also about writing and knowing what to discard. I've produced a lot of rubbish in my time – but so has everyone, which is why it makes a great subject for an anthology.

John Greening

Small finds

What's left of anyone is the unchosen.
If I could choose, it would be these:
a Belgian bottle opener, a demob trunk,
a ruby necklace and a wooden-handled paring knife.

And I would have a boat grave,
sleeping in my long steel shell
till excavators found me, disappointed by
my legacy of swarf and fire cement.

My archaeology will be a raggedy assemblage
of spiral wires from notebook spines,
the barrel of a plastic fountain pen split like a bone
for marrow; nothing much to show.

Jo Bell

The Apotheosis of the Garbagemen

And they come back in the night through alleys to find us
By the clashing of raised lids,
By garage doors' lifted heads, the swung gates, the bottomless
Galvanized cans on their shoulders,
In luminous coveralls
They follow the easy directions on boxes, scattering
Bushels of brown grass and apple cores,
Old candy wrappers folded around sweet nothings,
And sacks with their stains on fire,
They are coming through hedges, dragging geometry
In a dark clutch of rainbows,
See, the smashed jars
Prinked out with light, and the vacuum bags
Bursting their dust in the night like the phantasms of horseflies,
Through the burning bacon fat
Their baseball caps go flying, their feet
As solid as six-packs on the lawn, the slam-bang of their coming
Sending the lettuce leaves against our windows
Like luna moths, the marrow whistling
Out of the wishbones of turkeys, the husks and rinds,
The lost-wax castings of corncobs and teabags,
The burnt-out lightbulbs pulsing in midair,
The coupons filled out
With our last names for all the startling offers,
Oh see, their hands are lifted by the gloves
Untying the knots in plastic bags, to catch
The half-burnt ashes raining around their heads,
The crusts and empties.
As the skeletons of lampshades catch at the first light,
They are going back in their empty trucks and singing
To the dump, to the steaming rust
In the rolling, hunch-backed, beckoning earth,
The sea of decay where our foundering fathers
Rubbled their lives,

They have found the way
Back to God's plenty, to rags and riches,
But will come back to us with all we could wish for
In the darkness, singing love and wild appetite,
The good rats and roaches,
The beautiful hogs and billygoats dancing around them.

David Wagoner (1926 – 2021)

Swing-bin

Furled white plastic,
last limp flag on a roll,
this bin-liner (swing, not pedal)
was painlessly separated
along the perforations provided.

Its sides swell now with peelings.
Tea-bags wilt into crannies.
Crumbs of seed-cake dust
the surface with stale pollen
(my mother's tested recipe).

A roll-on deodorant
nudges old rags aside; torn
envelopes, a twist of string
(the kind my father used
to make us kites as children).

Litter of garlic-husk
confetti (to please my husband
once a week on Fridays);
your tapes: rich swill of
Beethoven, Monteverdi,
Katja Kabanova; spaghetti maggots
slide with the subterranean
tremor of springing leaves.

Susan Wicks

Landfill Cell Remediation

GENII LOCI

The cell is shaped to mimic nearby hills,
a pregnant bank the monitoring wells
fathom for unfounded growth,
black liquid accumulations.
A pump sighs in the long grass.
Then another in a clump of sorrel.
More down by the nesting box,
until the cell's a hill of sighs, each well
a source of loss, a ghost knelt
listening to its own dead breath
as it tends cracked yoghurt cartons, crockery,
things fallen out of reach –
beneath thistledown snagged on an old LP
the midden's black placenta throbs.

John Wedgwood Clarke

House Clearance

When you were gone, widow in a childless house,
As smoke, as shadow of smoke and thin deposit of ash
Forgive us, we went from room to room under the roofspace
Lagged with woolly dust, under that head of cold
We gathered up your substance, all the leavings
And sorted this for us, this for charity, this for the tip
Breaking and entering on your privacy
We delved for what you might have hoarded among underwear
The orange chocolate biscuits, wallets of photographs
Wads of pension, documentations of a dead baby,
Hardening our hearts, impieties, impieties,
Even against the cards heart-shaped and red and quilted
Addressed to MAM from someone not your flesh
For Christmas, birthday and Mothering Sunday
That being opened down a score of years still chimed
Like mobiles in a wreck, but we
With coats and hats more than in C&A
More dresses than a run of Mothers' Union jumble sales
With orange cardigans and the summer blouses
That crush to nothing like a conjuror's bright scarves
We bloated the first black plastic bags
The grey dust in our hair, and rounded up
From where you had hidden them or they hid themselves
In hide-and-seek and nobody came seeking
The last of your rag and woolly tribe of dolls and animals
Already priced for charity, room by room until
From a wardrobe out flopped
A clown the size of a boy of five or six
Sewn in motley, stuffed and grinning, right as ninepence
And we blessed you for that, for giving us a thing
At once we could give away to the girl next door who asked,
Now you are gone, Was the house haunted? Yes, by love.

David Constantine

Rubbish!
for Jane

You'll say it if I'm being doctrinaire,
or when you're watching *Question Time*. But once
your early morning walk's begun, the hunt's
for literal litter. What's that bloody smear?
A Burger King usurped. Who chucked this beer?
Flat denial. Mask. Condom. Each offence
attended to with bright blue latex hands
while I'm not even dressed, but in my chair,
directing screwed-up poems at the basket:
a mile off, Larkin! And wondering, should I
just clear them all ... yet thinking too of Brahms
who said it's what you drop beneath your desk
that makes the symphony. *Rubbish!* you cry.
Your resolution, and your outstretched arms.

John Greening

This Is a Hymn
for Michael Granzen

For all who ride the trains
all night,
sleep on sidewalks and park benches
beneath basements
and abandoned buildings
this is a hymn.
For those whose homes
are the great outdoors
the streets their one big room,
for live men asleep in tombs
this is a hymn.

This is a hymn for bag women
pushing rubbish babies
in ridiculous prams,
dividing open lots
into elaborate architects' plans.

Mansions of the dispossessed,
magnificence of desperate rooms,
kings and queens of homelessness
die with empty bottles
rising from their tombs.

This a hymn
for all recommending
a bootstrap as a way
to rise with effort
on your part.
This is a hymn,
may it renew
what passes for your heart.

This hymn
is for the must-be-blessed
the victims of the world
who know salt best.
The world tribe
of the dispossessed
outside the halls of plenty
looking in,
this is a benediction
this is a hymn.

Lorna Goodison

Report from an Island

Sea washes the sands in a frill of salt and a *yes* sound.
We lie beneath palms, under the star constellations

of the global south: a cross, a sword pointing upward.
Through frangipani trees, a light wind. Bats foraging.

Foreigners smoke the bats out by burning coconuts,
calling this *the bat problem*. Or they set out poisonous fruit.

The gecko hides under a banana leaf. So far nothing is said.
A gecko mistaken for a bird that sings in the night.

It is no bird. A healer blows smoke into the wound.
Sees through flesh to a bone once broken.

In the sea, they say, there is an island made of bottles and other trash.
Plastic bags become clouds and the air a place for opportunistic birds.

One and a half million plastic pounds make their way there every hour.
The pellets are eggs to the seabirds, and the bags, jellyfish to the turtle.

So it is with diapers, shampoo, razors and snack wrappers, soda rings
and six-pack holders. Even the sacks to carry it all home flow to the sea.

Wind has lofted the water into a distant city, according to news reports:
most of that city submerged now, with fish in the streets.

It is no bird. The man hasn't sold any of his carved dolphins.
Geckos don't sing. The vendor of sarongs hasn't sold a single one.

Prau, the boats are called throughout this archipelago.
Spider-looking. Soft-motored. Waiting at dawn.

Geckos can't blink, so they lick their own eyes to keep them wet. Their bite
is gentle, they eat mealworms and crickets. This is why no crickets sing.

No one talks about it, but people look to the sea
toward where the plane went down. There is time to imagine:

one hundred eighty-nine souls buckled to their seats on the seafloor,
the wind too much for the plane, the gecko now at the door.

After the earthquake, people moved into the family tombs.
Many graves now have light and running water.

Others live at the dumps in trash cities, where there is work sorting
plastic, metal, glass, tantalum from cell phones and precious earths.

This work is slow. A low hum of ordinary life drills into the mind
like the sound of insects devouring a roof. There is no hope for it.

There is only the sea and its *yes*, lights in the city of the dead,
and a plastic island that must from space appear to be a palace.

Carolyn Forché

Learning to Listen on the Thames Beach
for Mimi

I like to look; you tell me I must also listen.
I scan the beach for iron and try to listen.

Tide holds for just so long then drops its flotsam –
mudlarking's in my blood: I'll try to listen.

The stones, nails, shoes, this one old mitten;
they all could have some meaning if I listen.

Sky that gulls love, the lukewarm sun of Whitsun,
only stand for what they are; unless I listen.

The river arcs its back, its lyric's written,
sings the song of tides to those who listen.

As night draws in and the birds of Hackney quieten
know that Anna sits in Lambeth trying to listen.

Anna Robinson

The Burning of the Leaves

Now is the time for the burning of the leaves.
They go to the fire; the nostril pricks with smoke
Wandering slowly into a weeping mist.
Brittle and blotched, ragged and rotten sheaves!
A flame seizes the smouldering ruin and bites
On stubborn stalks that crackle as they resist.

The last hollyhock's fallen tower is dust;
All the spices of June are a bitter reek,
All the extravagant riches spent and mean.
All burns! the reddest rose is a ghost;
Sparks whirl up, to expire in the mist: the wild
Fingers of fire are making corruption clean.

Now is the time for stripping the spirit bare,
Time for the burning of days ended and done,
Idle solace of things that have gone before:
Rootless hope and fruitless desire are there;
Let them go to the fire, with never a look behind.
The world that was ours is a world that is ours no more.

They will come again, the leaf and the flower, to arise
From squalor of rottenness into the old splendour,
And magical scents to a wondering memory bring;
The same glory, to shine upon different eyes.
Earth cares for her own ruins, naught for ours.
Nothing is certain, only the certain spring.

Laurence Binyon (1869 – 1943)